I0490886

JOSEF STETTER
AWARD-WINNING AUTHOR, SPEAKER AND GUINNESS WORLD RECORD PARTICIPANT

Secrets to Landing Your Dream Job Revealed

Legal Disclaimer

Copyright © 2023 JOSEF STETTER. All rights reserved worldwide.

No part of this material may be used, reproduced, distributed or transmitted in any form and by any means whatsoever, including without limitation photocopying, recording or other electronic or mechanical methods or by any information storage and retrieval system, without the prior written permission from the author, except for brief excerpts in a review. This book is intended to provide general information only. Neither the author nor publisher provides any legal or other professional advice. If you need professional advice, you should seek advice from the appropriate licensed professional. This book does not provide complete information on the subject matter covered. This book is not intended to address specific requirements, either for an individual or an organization. This book is intended to be used only as a general guide and not as a sole source of information on the subject matter. While the author has undertaken diligent efforts to ensure accuracy, there is no guarantee of accuracy or of no errors, omissions or typographical errors. Any slights of people or organizations are unintentional. The author and publisher shall have no liability or responsibility to any person or entity and hereby disclaim all liability, including without limitation, liability for consequential damages regarding any claim, loss or damage that may be incurred, or alleged to have been incurred, directly or indirectly, arising out of the information provided in this book.

Connect with Magnetic Entrepreneur Inc.™
https://www.facebook.com/magneticentrepreneur
www.linkedin.com/in/magneticentrepreneur
E-Mail: magneticpublishing2017@gmail.com
Website: www.magnetic-entrepreneur.com

Copyright © 2023 by JOSEF STETTER
All rights reserved. No part of this publication may be reproduced or transmitted in any form or by any means, electronic, or mechanical, including photocopying, recording, or by any information storage and retrieval system.

DEDICATION

A very special thank you to my amazing wife, Adi Stetter, for supporting and believing in my dreams and igniting my fire to give back and support our ever-growing family. I love you with all my heart, and thank you for all you do for our family. Thank you for gifting one of my biggest dreams of becoming a father to an incredibly funny and talented daughter Mia Zohar. I am so excited to grow our family with more amazing children.

Acknowledgements

To the incredible mentors who have taken the time to share their wisdom, insights and expertise, no words can describe my gratitude for your time and guidance. You have shown me what is possible and how to play bigger and continue to expose me to new opportunities. I love and admire you all, including but not limited to Robert J Moore, Dr. Obom Bowen, Loral Langemeier, Opher Brayer and more!

TABLE OF CONTENTS

Contents

FOREWORD

A true expert in his field is one who shares his knowledge and skills with others and teaches them how to succeed. Josef Stetter is just that person and more.

He has not only succeeded in his field and obtained his dream job, but he has helped over 11,000 people find a job they love in under three months. His success rate in recruitment stands at an amazing 90% in finding anyone employment in any field with his proven systems.

He amassed this expertise over the course of switching careers nine times and 17 jobs. Because of his wide range of experience, he has developed and taught advanced strategies that maximize results for finding that elusive job for which his clients are searching.

Having a coach like Josef who ensures you stand out and get noticed by those responsible for hiring when you submit your resume and cover letter makes the process so much easier, with a positive result.

Not only does Josef provide his insights on what an employer is looking for in a job candidate, but he also prepares the job searcher for the interview, coaching them to give them the confidence in salary negotiation when they are offered the job.

In addition to his coaching courses, Josef is also an Award-Winning and International Best-Selling Author in Canada and the USA of *Congratulations You Are Hired: It Was Easier Than You Thought.* Josef also published four other books and is an Award-Winning Speaker and Guinness World Record Participant. The testimonials included in this book attest to the powerful results Josef is able to achieve for his clients.

Josef's ability to clearly communicate his strategies provides the opportunity and the inspiration to pursue and land YOUR dream job!

Robert J. Moore

5x International Awarded Author

CEO and Founder of Magnetic Entrepreneur Inc.™

INTRODUCTION

Josef Stetter has coached and trained over 11,000 job seekers and new immigrants on finding a job in their field. Using his techniques, he's had a 90% success rate for finding people jobs within three months.

What makes this astonishing is that these people had no Canadian experience, or had criminal records, or disabilities, and had been regular job seekers at all levels. It was Josef's coaching that made the difference. Whether the economy is good or bad, there are jobs available. Your success comes down to how well you market yourself, how well you make yourself stand out.

Josef has successfully helped people find work in all industries, including Construction, Engineering, Education, Human Resources (HR), Information Technology (IT), Pharmaceutical, Marketing, Project Management and Sales. It doesn't matter what industry or position you seek; if you have the specific technical knowledge for the job and the passion, it's all about who you are. What you bring to the table is the same for any job in any industry.

Here are a couple of examples to illustrate this point.

Josef's brother was finishing his third year of mechanical engineering studies and had applied for an internship. However, by the time the company responded with an interview, he'd already registered for his fourth year. He decided he no longer wanted the job. So, he asked Josef to cancel the interview.

As a career coach, Josef thought this would be a great way to personally try out his 7-step program. Josef went to the interview as his brother. Keep in mind; he had no engineering knowledge; his background was in economics and business. All he knew was what he had written on his brother's resume.

In the first interview, he was in competition with more than 100 engineering students from four universities. Within forty-five minutes, the company called to ask if he'd meet with the hiring manager. During the meeting, Josef simply repeated what he knew from his brother's resume. For example, his brother had been on a team that designed a wheelchair for third world nations that uses a tank chain and, therefore, can go on any terrain. The project won second prize in Ontario for the best mechanical engineering project of the year, along with a $500 prize from the Royal Bank of Canada. Josef also told the manager his brother had studied quantum physics and thermal dynamics, even though Josef himself had no clue what those were.

Fifteen minutes after the interview, the manager called him to say he wanted Josef to come in for a third and final interview. Out of the one-hundred initial candidates, Josef – a non-engineer – made it to the final three.

The next morning, he was first to arrive at 8:30 a.m. sharp. The manager came over and said, "Congratulations, this is your letter of offer. All you have to do is pass this mechanical engineering test." After repeatedly looking at the test and the manager, Josef finally said, "I'm sorry, but I cannot do this test. I guess I'm a lot more comfortable with design than I am with calculations."

"I'm not the right candidate for you. I'm truly sorry for wasting your time." The manager replied, "I know you're nervous; let me help you." He then proceeded to give Josef answers to the first three questions.

Amazed, Josef responded, "I'm flattered, but I cannot take this job. I'm not the right candidate." The manager followed Josef to his car and begged him to take the job, arguing he interviewed so much better than all the other engineers.

Without any engineering skills and by simply using his own seven-step interview technique, Josef stood out above far more technically qualified candidates and could have landed the job.

Another example of how effective Josef's 7-step technique is was illustrated when Josef and a friend were discussing a new job she wanted. However, believing she was severely under-qualified, she thought she had no chance of landing the job. Josef suggested she try his seven-step program. At first, she resisted. After all, she thought, "How could his predefined 7-step interviewing process make up for a lack of technical qualification?"

Fortunately, Josef persisted, and as he described his seven-step program, she began to realize its value. As a result, and along with Josef's suggestions for modifying her resume, not only was she interviewed, but within two weeks was offered the job! They told her she was the best candidate out of more than 100 they had interviewed.

The position had been open for over six months, and no one had ever come close to passing the second interview with eight people from different departments.

Thanks to Josef's coaching and his techniques, his friend was able to amaze them, managing the various personality types effectively and having them all agree she was indeed the right person for the job.

Now, readers can discover Josef's 7-step technique and more by simply reading this book.

Good luck with your career.

Josef Stetter

Preface

Why should you buy this book?

This book is not about teaching you more of what you know; it's about ensuring you know how to stand out above the competition; by using proven tools and techniques that will get you noticed in any industry for any job in any economy. It's about tweaking and refining your approach to find the perfect job for you!

"Find a job you like, and you add five days to every week."

- H. Jackson Browne

Many qualified and capable individuals have found themselves scrambling to find any job they can, willing to settle for anything just to make ends meet. After a few negative experiences, many start having fears and doubts, so much so they lose sight of who they are! How does this affect them? Do they start playing it safe and safer and safer to avoid getting hurt? Do they give up their dreams and their passions? Do they throw out their laughter, their joy and their self-expression?

If you're like me, as the bills pile up and your confidence in your abilities diminishes, you may get stuck in a vicious circle of failure and disappointment forgetting why you were good at what you did. Having a unique resume, being able to wow your interviewer, looking for work in the right places and focusing your energy will only result in success.

Most people feel completely drained and uninspired when their job search has continued over a certain period of time. Do you know them? Have you been one? Do you feel completely stopped in one or several areas of your life for days, weeks, months and even years! Want to know how to get unstuck from this disastrous draining wheel of life?

To regain your confidence.

To bring back your passion for your work.

To take a leap of faith better than you could have imagined.

Why don't more people take this leap of faith? Why do so many keep making the same mistakes? Why do so many all have the same cookie-cutter resume, answer most interview questions with the same textbook answers, and email blast their resume everywhere? What do you think happens? Life happens, life gets in the way of living, and they get stuck on the wheel of life.

Most people have heard of the 80-20 rule, but they don't really understand it. It's simple; the majority of unemployed individuals are looking at 20% of the jobs and then throw their hands up in the air in frustration as they feel they can't find anything. By adding flavour and personality, you'll have confidence, and you'll get noticed!

We get stuck in routines and responsibilities that prevent us from fulfilling our dreams. We play it safe instead of taking a leap of faith and truly believing in our talents and abilities. We spend hours online looking for a job instead of pounding the pavement and going to talk to people. We settle for less than what we are destined to do.

How different would your life look if you took the leap of faith and just followed your dreams? Just imagine how happy you would be, doing what you love and making a living at it.

We live in a world where innovation and creativity are the key components of implementing change and redefining the existing business model.

"Be a yardstick of quality. Some people aren't used to an environment where excellence is expected." - Steve Jobs

Following your dreams should especially hold true for what you do for a living, as you spend a majority of your life doing it. You need to show you have value to offer, and you bring something to the table that no one else can offer. Oprah Winfrey said: *"You know you're on the road to success if you would do your job and not be paid for it."* This book will bring to light just what an important role you play in getting work done efficiently and effectively to help a company grow and increase overall profits.

"The biggest mistake that you can make is to believe that you are working for somebody else. Job security is gone. The driving force of a career must come from the individual. Remember: Jobs are owned by the company; you own your career!"

Earl Nightingale

CHAPTER 1:
WHAT! PASSION IS WORTH MORE THAN MONEY?

Purpose

It wouldn't be fair if I kept my knowledge and my insights on the art and science of job finding to myself.

When it came to knowing and pursuing my purpose and my passion, I was clueless, and therefore over the past 25 years, I have switched careers about nine times and have held about 18 jobs. Each time, I had to go through the trials and tribulations of "customizing a resume" and proving I had the transferable skills required, and the certainty I was perfect for a role only to be rejected and passed up, and the need to prove myself repeatedly.

I have worked at various jobs over the years just to pay the bills, never believing anything else was possible or that what I enjoy doing is truly my calling – until I got into recruitment. More than anything, I wanted the approval of my parents, who could not understand my desire for passion while maximizing my earning potential.

I grew up in a family that was risk-averse. A "good job" was the expected norm, especially with a father who was a Civil Engineer that grew up in communist Romania and a

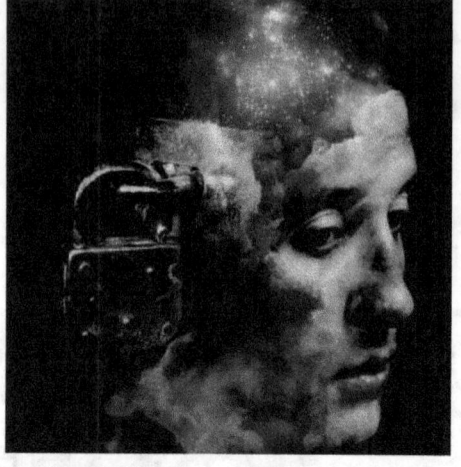

mother who was a teacher, two jobs that have been in demand for the 30 years I have lived in Canada.

My parents' mindset was simple: people work for 35 years at the same job and then retire. For them, it was about stability and security rather than passion. Most of my life has felt like a yo-yo, with two steps forward and five steps back.

If Passion Was Eternal – Where Would I Focus?

Passion

Helping other people has always been my primary driver, sharing in their success stories, sharing in their achievements.

They say the universe only gives you what you can handle, and I have come out stronger and better every time I learned from failure and let me tell you, have I failed.

I failed because I worked many jobs that paid me but didn't excite me, which caused me undue stress and was costing me my health and overall mental well-being. How many of you feel lost, angry and frustrated with a job that doesn't fulfill you?

To change your life, you must make progressive steps. You don't need all the answers to achieve the end goal; you just need to set the goal! Even if you figure out exactly what you want to do, something else will happen — life happens and gets in the way of living, and we get stuck or run in circles trying to find the right path to success; something always happens.

There is no straight line to success, and the road is always under construction. You want to be excited and motivated to go to work every day and feel like you made a difference in someone's life at the end of it. This experience is not a job – it is a life's fulfillment, your career fulfillment. That is why I have made it my life mission to help you land your dream job and get paid what you are worth and more.

https://www.facebook.com/groups/Landyourdreamjob2020/

CHAPTER 2:
IN PURSUIT OF MY DREAM JOB –
I CAN HELP YOU LAND YOURS

Navigating the abyss of job finding is about clear focus, and we can achieve your success story together.

When I know I've made a difference in a person's career; there is no greater achievement that I can add to my list of accomplishments. Helping people navigate through what appears to be the abyss of job finding, now more than ever is a priority that can no longer take a back seat to other endeavours.

Pursuit

FOCUS on the right career. Ensure **FUSION** of the right key terms and results you have produced.

Achieve **FULFILLMENT** in landing your dream job

I want to empower you and help you recognize that opportunities exist in all markets and economies. I want you to feel inspired and to know that there are companies that will desire and appreciate your talents, skills and ability to produce results. These are the companies you want to work with.

I want to share the over 25,000 hours of practical and theoretical learning that makes up the psychology, the algorithms, the systems and the tools to secure your next job. I have helped almost 11,000 job seekers find their dream job, and there are millions more around the world that need my help.

I have designed the perfect formula to help you navigate through these economically challenging times.

https://www.facebook.com/groups/Landyourdreamjob2020/

What Qualifies Me, And What Differentiates Me?

During my entire professional life, I have solved the mystery of getting hired in any field in any economy.

I'm a people connector, and this ability allows me to shine a light on anyone and have them recognized for their value and contributions. I've been able to diminish the anxiety of uncertainty when awaiting responses and ultimately getting hired faster and more strategically.

I have multiple levels of insights, systems and techniques that I've spent 25,000 hours mastering. There isn't a job seeker I haven't been able to help; regardless of cultural background, experience, having a criminal record, having any form of disability, I have helped them all! As a matter of fact, I have done the exact same thing for myself 18 times with different industries, at different levels from entry to leadership, in different locations and in multiple countries.

Possibility

I have also recruited for small to global companies in a multitude of industries such as Tata Consulting Services, IBM, Deloitte & Touché, Apotex Pharmaceuticals, Leo Pharmaceuticals, Aecon Construction, CapitalOne Financial and many more.

I want every job seeker to have hope and experience the ease of transitioning to a better opportunity for themselves! With my 90% success rate, rate, job seekers will land their dream job in under three months, in some cases, two days!

What's The Main Reason That I Go To Work Every Day?

I've always wanted to be appreciated and valued in the job(s) I held, and that doesn't always equate to money.

In 2006, I became an entrepreneur by opening up my own employment agency after generating over $760,000 for another recruitment firm (five times more than any other employee) the previous year, earning little to no commission for my contributions and getting cheese and crackers as my Christmas bonus. It wasn't about the cheese and crackers, as much as it was, how I felt – little to no appreciation for me and my efforts. Unfortunately, this lack of appreciation is very common, which is why it's so important that you land your dream job!

Shortly after, I felt so defeated that I quit that job and spent the next three months focusing on my entrepreneurship efforts. My business was making me more than triple what I had earned as an employee with commissions and bonuses. I didn't think the money would ever stop coming in, so I didn't worry about contingency planning and diversifying my revenue streams.

Performance

During the first two and a half years, everything I touched turned to gold, and I was spending everything I earned with no cares in the world. I lived way beyond my means as money kept pouring in. I needed to 'show-off' my wealth by treating everyone to dinners and drinks, buying expensive toys, and more. I was young and was  thoroughly enjoying the concept of being an entrepreneur.

In 2010, my business did a complete 180, and the next eight and a half years were a constant struggle. The market crashed, and my three biggest clients downsized approximately 1500 people each. I went from having 60 to 80 orders a month to having

none overnight. To make things worse, all three of my biggest clients put a three-year freeze on hiring. The market was flooded with professionals that lost their jobs, and none of my clients needed my services anymore.

We are now in the midst of a global pandemic where people are being downsized again, and the need to stand out above the rest is more important than ever! There will be at least 5 to 10 times more  competition for roles, and that's why it's important that you have the critical information on how to get noticed, stand out above the competition and get hired.

The best strategy is the one that includes truly pursuing the role and the responsibilities that will motivate you and drive you to exceed your own objectives each and every day.

What Have I Learned, and How Can I Teach Others?

Sometimes we think that nothing can ever go wrong until it all goes wrong and then some.

My former business partner stole over $180,000 from me, and as a result, I got stuck with a $93,000 tax bill (corporate, personal, CPP, and EI) for a total debt of over $273,000.

When you owe taxes to the government, you can't declare bankruptcy as the government can garnish up to 90% of your earnings, which means you can't afford things like rent, car and more. Even worse, the government charges 29.99% interest in penalties, which is  accrued in a compounded monthly equation, which means you are only paying interest if you pay the minimum.

I've had debts before, but nothing this astronomical. I was crushed! I was depressed, I was lost. I had to move back in with my parents, which only reminded me how much I had failed. This made my reality even worse as my parents were disappointed in me, embarrassed by me and treated me like a hardened criminal! The sense of feeling worthless is something I don't want any job seeker to feel. I achieved all that success and had nothing (a very large negative) to show for it.

How would you feel if your employer told you they were sorry, but all your capabilities were not needed anymore? I'm sure many of you have gone through this! That is why I am committed to empowering you and getting you back on track as quickly and efficiently as possible.

Perspective

While I was experiencing the worst time of my life, my father, my hero and mentor, passed away from both leukemia and heart problems. He passed seeing his son fail and worried whether I would ever find my way. I love and miss him dearly. He taught me so much, and I truly believe he is guiding me and protecting me from above. It has also reminded me how precious life is and how little time we spend appreciating what we have and those around us.

This picture of my father holding my first nephew brought him so much joy during his suffering. I do not want people to suffer, especially not in a job that makes them miserable, which ultimately leads to other stressful life situations. This is why I've created this program — link can be found here:

https://www.facebook.com/groups/Landyourdreamjob2020/

Chapter 3:
The Past Formulates Our Present

My past and the lessons learned prepared me for right now!

Today, I'm so proud to say I have a clean slate and erased my entire debt of $285,000 after eight and a half very trying

years. I am surrounded by amazing, inspiring mentors and friends. I know what is possible and allow myself to dream bigger than I ever have. I married the love of my life in June, 2019, and we are expecting our first child, a daughter, on May 30th, 2020. I can't wait to be a father; my family is my WHY! I want you to have the best opportunities for your WHY.

Presence

As an entrepreneur, I realize that challenges will come in different ways and at different times. There is the struggle to generate income, the need to re-invent yourself, the need to stay ahead of the competition and the need to learn new skills like social media marketing. All of these apply to landing your dream job and advancing your career.

The economy is cyclical and always has booms and recessions. Unfortunately, this is the beginning of a nasty recession because of  Covid-19. The landscape and the way business is being conducted are universally changing. You need and want to stand out above the competition. It is crucial that you believe in yourself. The universe will provide you with all of your heart's desires if you focus your thoughts and energy on gratitude, the positives, and the desire to be of service to others. This IS OUR TIME!

https://www.facebook.com/groups/Landyourdreamjob2020/

Giving Up Is Easy But Not The Right Option

I wanted to give up, but I didn't quit because I believed in myself.

Persistence

My $285,000 lesson forced me to be resourceful, find mentors, join masterminds, and create a tribe that continues to grow. I even took on more debt to go back to school for another career change — to become a high school educator that does everything in his power to inspire his students to learn, grow and achieve success. You must be willing to pay the price, to put in your time, and to learn from mentors how to enjoy the fruits of your success, experience and expertise. You learn there is no failure — only lessons, results and feedback.

It takes persistence, resilience, and a fighting spirit to achieve anything you want in life! We seldom know the day or the hour that our desires and passions will come true, but the chance that you will create the moment is possible if you don't quit.

When you find and align with great mentors and people that cheer you on, success will be closer than you ever imagined. Make failure your friend. I'm here to tell you that the tough times are exactly when your story gets interesting. Without the darkness, how would you know the light? How would you know what you are truly capable of if everything was easy? My desire is to become a mentor to millions, including you, and help everyone find the perfect role with the perfect company.

I have risen from the ashes like a phoenix, and having mentors who truly care has made the biggest difference in my life. I want to be your mentor and celebrate your success!

https://www.facebook.com/groups/Landyourdreamjob2020/

How Does My Program Make A Difference To You?

I've helped almost 11,000 job seekers land their dream job and want to make a difference in your job search too!

Proactivity

Whether the economy is good or bad, there are always jobs available. Your success comes down to how well you market yourself, how well you make yourself stand out and how proactive you are consistently.

A couple stories that stand out include Tina and Robert.

I met Tina in 2017. Tina was in a severe car accident that prevented her from being able to work for over a year and a half. She was depressed and lost all confidence in her ability to find work. This carried over into her personal life as she felt she was not contributing enough to her partner, which nearly cost her the one thing that brought her joy. She had been sending resumes for over four months with no response.

Life was at a standstill, and she felt no one wanted to hire her because of her age; she was 53. After she joined my master training program, wrote her resume, revamped her LinkedIn profile and was taught how to interview, she was hired as a Social Media Manager for the most successful Ford dealership in Ontario, Canada. We are still friends to this day, and I helped her land a new role in mid-2019 when her previous leadership changed, and her work environment became very toxic.

Professionalism

I was introduced to Robert by a friend in 2013. We met for coffee, and he explained to me that he had been sending out resumes and getting little to no response. His bills were piling up, and he was stressing about the possibility of moving back home with his parents after being independent for over 12 years. He spoke with such passion about being an electrical engineer. I invited him to take advantage of the master training program to secure his dream job. He agreed, and within a few short weeks, he had multiple offers, something he had never experienced in his career.

Chapter 4: How Do I Save You a 15- to 30- Year Learning Curve?

There are no shortcuts to success but teaching you what I've already learned allows you to have a great head start!

This program is about innovation, teaching you how to stand out while leveraging the knowledge you already have and the knowledge you will gain. By using proven tools and techniques, you will pave the way to your goals, your successes and ultimately, your overall motivations.

Practicality

Many qualified and capable individuals have found themselves scrambling to find any job they can, willing to settle for anything just to make ends meet. I've been there. After a few negative experiences, many start having fears and doubts, so much so that they lose sight of who they are!

If you're like me, as the bills pile up and your confidence in your abilities diminishes, you may get stuck in a vicious circle of failure and disappointment, forgetting why you were so good at what you did. Having a unique resume, being able to wow the

interviewer, looking for work in the right places and focusing your energy where your passion lies will always result in success. Do you want to know how to get unstuck from this disastrous draining wheel of life?

TRANSFORM YOURSELF!

How Are You Spending The 24 Hours In Your Day?

Most people have heard the 80/20 rule, but very few understand it.

Percentage

It's simple; most unemployed individuals are looking at 20% of the jobs and then give up as they feel they can't find anything. By adding flavor and personality, while uncovering hidden job search gems, you'll have the confidence to get noticed, and more importantly, you will get hired!

How different would life look like if you took the leap of faith and had a system that guarantees results? Just imagine how happy you would be, doing what you love and making a living at it. We live in a world where innovation and creativity are the key components of implementing change and redefining the existing business model.

This system will show you what an important role you play in getting work done efficiently and effectively to help a company grow and increase overall profits. This is a total system, not just complex theories. If you want to be hired, this system is a must! It is a system that will give you the A to Z of job finding, complete with live training and loads of extras.

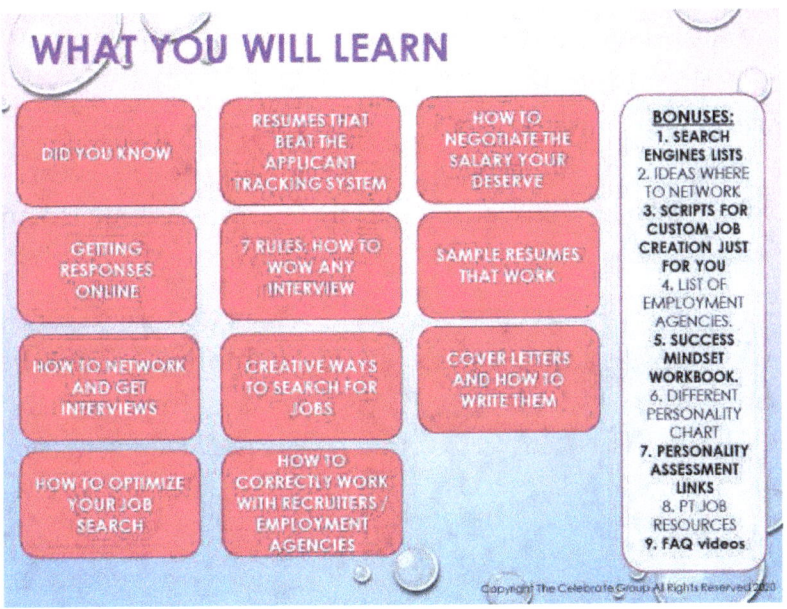

Is There Someone Who Won't Succeed In My Program?

With so many gimmicks out there, the real proof is in the tried, and tested systems learned through actual experience.

If you want the simple answer to the question above, the answer is NO. Everyone can succeed, and the only reason people fail is that they do not commit to the system, the tools and the techniques. Remember, there are no shortcuts to success!

Proof

Here are two examples:

My brother was finishing his third-year mechanical engineering program and had applied for an internship. However, by the time the company responded with an interview, he'd already registered for his fourth year. He decided he no longer wanted the job. So, he asked me to cancel the interview.

As a career coach, I thought this would be a great way to personally try out my 7-step program. I went to the interview as my brother. Keep in mind; I had no engineering knowledge; my background was in economics and business. All I knew was what I had written on my brother's resume.

In the first interview, I was competing against 100 engineering students. Within forty-five minutes, the company called to ask if I'd meet with the hiring manager. And during the final interview, I had made it to the final three.

The next morning, I was first to arrive, and the manager came over and said, "Congratulations, this is your letter of offer. All you have to do is pass this mechanical engineering test." After repeatedly looking at the test and the manager, I apologized to  him and told him I couldn't do the test. I told him I was more comfortable with design than calculations and that I wasn't the right candidate for the company. The manager told me I interviewed better than any of the other candidates and went the extra effort to convince me to reconsider.

When my friend told me that she wanted a new job as an Environmental Technician, she believed she was severely under-qualified as she was working as a Museum Program Coordinator. She thought she had no chance of landing

the job. I suggested she try my seven-step interview program and customized resume. At first, she resisted since she thought it was impossible to make up for her lack of technical qualification.

Fortunately, I persisted and described my 7-step program, and she began to realize its value. As a result, and along with my suggestions for modifying her resume, not only was she interviewed but within a few weeks, she was offered the job! They told her she was the best candidate out of more than 70 they had interviewed.

The position had been open for over six months, and no one had ever come close to passing the second interview with eight people from different departments.

Now, YOU can discover the proven techniques to land your dream job.

https://www.facebook.com/groups/Landyourdreamjob2020/

Is A Cookie-Cutter Approach Really The Answer?

Job seekers need to prove their worth, not just claim it!

The 5 Cardinal Sins In Your Resume

Your resume needs to tell YOUR story, including your overall skills, education and accomplishments. And since it's your story, the resume should be more than a cookie-cutter document, but rather a unique representation of who YOU are. Here are a few helpful tips:

The Font

You want to pass the Applicant Tracking Systems (ATS) by scoring high with your resume, and while the ATS does favour Times New Roman or Arial fonts, EVERYONE uses these very basic styles, and by 'following the crowd,' you could get lost in the abyss of sameness. QUICK TIP:

Prepare two (2) versions of your resume: 1. A more basic version for older databases like Monster; and 2. one with some personality and flair that you can send as an attachment. NOTE: Make sure it's a PDF file so that the formatting does not get distorted with different versions of MS Word.

The Bullet Points

When you use circles, squares, or arrows, it looks generic and sends a message of non-creativity, not only in preparing your resume but also in the way you develop ideas. Again, the ATS may not capture your resume, but developing different versions for different job boards and job opportunities is a good exercise.

Personality

The Skills/Career Summary

Generic subjective information should not be included in this section, for example, using words such as hardworking, dedicated, committed, team player etc., as these should already be assumed if you want the job you're applying for.

This section should include how unique you are and what/how you can offer value - add to the company to which you're applying. QUICK TIP: If you can show measurable and definitive results that helped your previous employers win business, save money, and improve efficiencies, then you can get creative; otherwise, focus on **PROVEN RESULTS!!**

The Chronological Or Functional Resume

It's important to decide if you want to prepare a chronological resume (a list of your work history in order of date, with your most recent position first) versus a functional resume (which focuses on your skills and experience when your work history isn't directly related to the job you're applying for and/or have employment gaps). QUICK TIP: If your most recent job is not relevant to the position you're applying for, DO NOT put it first on your resume.

Your Duties And Responsibilities

THE BIGGEST SIN OF ALL is listing your duties and responsibilities and not quantifying the **RESULTS** you produced. **RESULTS** are key to getting that first interview. Results that include % or $ or time stats, quotas reached, budgets balanced etc. are value-added in any resume.

Some Valuable Extras

Objective Statement

An objective statement is only useful if you make it about THEM, not you. For example, how you can make them more money or improve their efficiencies versus why you need the job. There is a lot to be said about the language and words used in any document.

File Type

Send PDF files versus Word files as a general rule, as the formatting can be drastically distorted depending on what Word version companies use in-house. Word files are also more likely to contain a virus, while the PDF format keeps your resume looking as you created it. Always be sure to use the requested format of the employer if one is recommended.

Spelling & Grammatical Errors

It is said that "To err is human…" Well, in the world of resumes, to err can be the very reason your resume gets placed in the 'no pile'. Always make sure you double-check our work and perhaps have someone else proofread it as a fresh set of eyes can catch things you might not. This is one of the most common oversights on a job seeker's resume.

Below is a typical Resume for an executive position.

VICE PRESIDENT OF OPERATIONS
Strategic Planning & Execution / Finance & Accounting Operations / Manufacturing Streamlining & Optimization

Highly accomplished and decisive senior executive with 20+ years of progressive financial and operations leadership experience in domestic and global Manufacturing, Importing, and Retail industries. Demonstrated success streamlining business operations including financial controls, budgets, strategic planning, performance measurement, production schedules, and staff development. Results-driven resourceful problem solver with proven track record of revenue and EBITDA growth.

CORE QUALIFICATIONS

- Leadership & Team Building
- Business Planning & Analytics
- Revenue Growth & Profitability
- System Implementations

- Global Financial Operations Management
- Growth Strategy & Staff Development
- Financial Analysis, Planning, & Reporting
- Global Supply Chain Management

- Brand Recognition
- Contract Negotiations
- Board Membership
- Customer Satisfaction

CAREER HIGHLIGHTS

- Led executive team directing vetting and selecting private equity investor, in alignment with strategic plan. Earned $40M to $120M and EBITDA 25% annually for Best Health Sportswear.
- Saved $5.5M in manufacturing costs within underperforming domestic operation for Spring Garden Apparel Company, Inc. Led turnaround via development of strategic integration plans including financial and operational initiatives negotiating with offshore contractors in China and Mexico.
- Increased revenue growth from $60M to $200M in 4 years for Maxxim Plastics, Inc. Expanded locations from 4 to 50 nationally.

PROFESSIONAL EXPERIENCE

BEST HEALTH SPORTSWEAR, Philadelphia, PA   0000 – Present
Largest manufacturer of women and men's performance apparel in the US generating $130M with operations in Mexico, Guatemala, China, and the US.

VICE PRESIDENT, OPERATIONS & PRODUCTION PLANNING

Manage domestic and international Production Planning and Operations with 18 direct / 350 indirect reports overseeing planning, forecasting, engineering costing, purchasing, inventory control, and facility management functions with $60M budget. Prepare and implement annual production plan for 1.4M units annually. Develop and implement 5-year strategic plans. Monitor finished goods and raw materials inventory management. Determine and distribute product segment daily sales and inventory reporting metrics. Vet and select private equity investors. Collaborate with private equity principles and various outside contractors. Serve as Operational Executive to Board of Directors in 0000. Secure and present operational and manufacturing reporting for quarterly Board meetings and monthly operations meeting with private equity investors.

- Implemented real time production schedules for 18 domestic Manufacturing departments with 350 employees achieving 98% to 100% on time shipping performance.
- Saved $650K annually in overtime by launching "Train the Trainer" program reducing turnover and increasing productivity.
- Negotiated and secured contractor manufacturing in Mexico and Guatemala increasing annual production units $500K. Reduced stopped orders 60% by implementing daily walk about process in manufacturing.
- Increased domestic capacity 25% via implementation of small order and sample sewing cells.
- Established reporting process and metrics maintaining inventory levels at 4.7M – 4.8M with revenue growth of 10% annually.
- Led preparation and presentation of manufacturing and operational due diligence data during 14-month private equity negotiation process.
- Key player in successful purchase of Dolfin Corporation, a swimwear manufacturer with $15M in annual revenue. Integrated operations into Best Health structure saving $1.1M.

Continued

CHAPTER 5:
JOB FINDING SITES

There are so many valuable resources and job-finding sites online across Canada and worldwide. Each site offers similar but different platforms based on specific jobs, companies and/or industries. Below is a list of job finding sites that you will find useful:

USA	CANADA
LINKEDIN.COM	LINKEDIN.COM
ZIPRECRUITER.COM	ZIPRECRUITER.CA
INDEED.COM	INDEED.CA
GLASSDOOR.COM	GLASSDOOR.CA
CAREERBUILDER.COM	CAREERBUILDER.CA
MONSTER.COM	MONSTER.CA
CAREERS.GOOGLE.COM	CAREERS.GOOGLE.CA
JOB.COM	JOB.CA
SIMPLYHIRED.COM	SIMPLYHIRED.CA
LINKUP.COM	(city)JOBSHOP.CA - add your city
LADDERS.COM	ALLSTARJOBS.CA
DICE.COM	WOWJOBS.CA
SNAG.COM	JOBBANK.GC.CA
US.JOBS	ELUTA.CA
USAJOBS.GOV	JOBBOOM.CA

CHAPTER 6:
HOW CAN YOU APPLY TO MY MENTORSHIP PROGRAM?

If you are serious about changing your future, it starts with today.

Taking steps to change your career direction, and ultimately your life is closer than you think.

All you have to do to apply for my program is watch a short video and fill out a three-question questionnaire on my Facebook Group (JobSeekersEmpowered).

If you qualify, you will be accepted into my master-level training system. Qualifications are based on your drive, your motivation and your commitment to moving towards landing your dream job.

I love ALL of you and know that your dream job is right in front of you. You might not know it yet, but you will!

https://www.facebook.com/groups/Landyourdreamjob2020/

CHAPTER 7:
TESTIMONIALS

Robert Zadeh, MASc, B.Eng.

Highly-trained and seasoned electrical engineer, focused on high-quality work with applicable profitable results. August 1, 2013, Robert was a client of Josef's.

"Josef Stetter , the author of the highly recommended "must-have" book, titled "CONGRATULATIONS YOU ARE HIRED: IT WAS EASIER THAN YOU THOUGHT," is one of the most innovative, articulate, and caring career counsellors and teachers that I have seen. Coming from a purely technical background with limited interpersonal skills, I learned lots of fine details about resume and letter writing, the interview process (including mock interviews), salary & benefits negotiation, and communications skills from him personally, and also from his book. I was hired immediately on the spot at two different companies in a span of two years. In addition, he is a very personable and approachable individual, always willing to help, advise, and answer my questions. With no hesitation, I strongly recommend Josef Stetter for any related job or career counselling and motivational talks."

We continue to remain friends after helping him land two positions with higher pay and more responsibility. He was recently downsized due to the Covid 19 virus and reached out again for additional support. I was happy to serve my lifetime member and have already assisted him on how to stand out to get interviews during the lockdown.

Haya came into my life when we were partnered to perform on the same Salsa team while I was living in Ottawa. She was young and full of energy with the most amazing smile. While practicing our choreography and having coffee after some intense practices, she mentioned that she had recently graduated from Animation 3D Rendering and Video Editing. She had been sending out resumes for six months and only had one unsuccessful interview. I gave her some free advice and job search tips, and then she asked to join my lifetime membership. After re-writing her resume to highlight her immense creativity and talent, while teaching her my proven formula to "wow" the interview, she had nine job interviews within two weeks and three job offers.

While we were dating, my now wife, Adi, worked with Autistic children, and was told her contract was not being renewed. My wife cried for two days, worried that she wouldn't be able to find another job. I reminded her that if I could help so many people land their dream job out there, that I would absolutely do the same for her. I wrote her resume, and within days, she received calls for interviews and subsequent job offers within two days. I trained her on my 7 rules to a "Wow interview system," and it worked; she received three better offers with more pay, and overall better benefits and opportunity.

I celebrate people every day and look forward to celebrating even more, including you. Here are some additional testimonials (on LinkedIn) from the wonderful people I have met and helped along the way (let's add you to this list):

Steve Whiteside Ph.D., PCC

Vice President International Business Development at CIBT Education Group, Inc. March 10, 2020, Steve was a client of Josef's.

"I can't talk highly enough about Josef! I worked with Josef on some employment coaching. Not only did I gain a lot of insight from Josef, but I felt very confident about some issues after we coved them, compared to before we spoke. Josef has many years of experience in the HR world, and it is obvious to anyone who does any work with him. I would highly recommend Josef if you need any employment or career coaching or if you just need to bounce some ideas off of him. He is skilled and amazingly helpful. Thanks, Josef! Steve Whiteside Ph.D. Inspiration By Design"

Justine Sterling

Coordinator, Programs and Services - Manulife Empowering Women to Employment Project at JobStart November 21, 2019, Justine wasa client of Josef's.

"We were so pleased to have Josef volunteer as a guest speaker with the Manulife Empowering Women to Employment Program at Jobstart. Josef delivered a fantastic workshop on a variety of job-search related topics, from how to beat ATS (Applicant Tracking System – otherwise known as job board), to networking effectively and even some tips on successful interview techniques. He was incredibly engaging as a presenter and was so receptive to all the participants' questions. Josef knows a ton about job searching and delivers the information in a clear and interesting way. I would definitely recommend Josef when it comes to needing advice on job searching!"

Liam Kearney

Strategic marketing professional producing results and bringing out the best in people. March 9, 2020, Liam was a client of Josef's

"After meeting Josef at an event. He guided me with redesigning my resume and on strategies for moving in to a new role and within 2 weeks I had moved into a role much more suited to me and with greater opportunity. Josef is great for connecting the dots and his book is a great resource too. I have also referred some people to him who he has helped out. I couldn't recommend Josef any more highly. He is full of energy and very positive and gets the job done."

Zeyn E.
Accomplished, Focused and Driven. August 24, 2013, Zeyn was a client of Josef's.

"Josef is an incredibly passionate speaker and coach who doesn't kid when it comes to results. He has on numerous occasions helped me to succeed in achieving and attaining my goals in business. He takes his time go over details to ensure you fully understand his teaching. His book is a one-of-a-kind reference guide you should not leave home without."

Ayna Bogdanova
Graphic designer
August 4, 2013, Ayna was a client of Josef's.

"Josef was a pleasure to deal with. His coaching was inspiring and to the point. Thanks to him, I got a three-month internship in a highly competitive selection process: instead of two or more interviews, I was accepted after one."

Boris Dehtiar
Sales & Marketing Professional open to new opportunities
October 4, 2016, Boris was a client of Josef's.

"A few years ago, Josef coached me on his Principles of Communicating with Management and Succeeding in Interviews. To this day, I use these principles for dealing with both upper management and with subordinates.

His principles have helped me excel during numerous occasions, both in my current role and when I was applying for new positions in the past. He is soft-spoken, he has an amazing communication style, and he is immensely experienced. I will not hesitate to recommend him to anyone looking to grow professionally within their existing role, or when applying for new positions. Boris Dehtiar Marketing Manager"

Maxine Silberg RD MPH

Registered Dietitian August 7, 2013, Maxine was a client of Josef's.

"Josef was a great help when I started job searching. He helped to break down the process, so it didn't seem like an overwhelming job. From resume formatting/writing to proper networking techniques, Josef gave me practical hands-on tools and skills that gave me the confidence to apply and approach potential employers. Throughout the process, Josef was available for a quick question or a chat when needed. His understanding of the job search process coupled with his easy-going, approachable personality really helped me to take it one step at a time until I found and landed the job I always wanted!"

Blair Mills

"Construction is our business. Exceptional service is what we do. Exceeding your expectations is our goal." July 11, 2013, Blair was a client of Josef's.

"Josef has the talent and expertise to offer you invaluable information on how to better understand the mindset of how you need to market yourself to get noticed plus how to conduct yourself in a job interview. Just think about your situation. What makes you unique and able to stand out against your competition? What are the key win, win ways to present yourself in an interview? Josef was an asset of my re-branding and re-education on this whole process, so much so that I was hired in short order as compared to my past previous traditional efforts. You owe it to yourself to get in contact with Josef right now!"

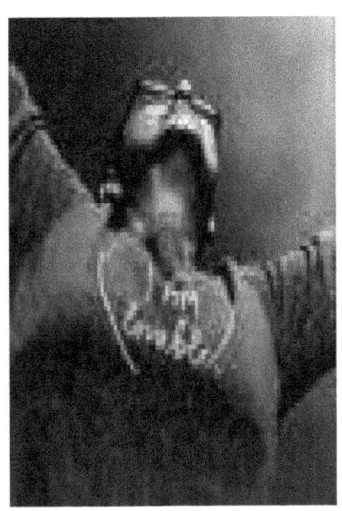

Wende Fahey
Spiritual Empowerment Coach and Block Therapy Student
March 27, 2012, Wende was a client of Josef's.

"Josef has helped me in many areas of my life, not just as a career coach. He comes from a place of high integrity and honesty. His approach is refreshing and different. He helped me get past a lot of my resistance to new ideas and to be present to the emotional upheaval that occurred while I moved through fear and reticence. He has helped me create new space in my life for my dreams. It's more like a conversation than coaching. I would highly recommend Josef for your career coaching needs! He's well-rounded, intelligent and quite frankly, a truly interesting and inspiring person. I can't thank him enough for the time he has spent with me!"

Charles Polanski
I help court reporters focus more time on reporting by polishing their transcripts via professional proofreading. August 24, 2011, Charles was a client of Josef's.

"Josef Stetter holds a treasure chest full of golden nuggets of knowledge on helping people get hired. His expertise and coaching helped me gain the confidence and competence to know I won't ever have to worry about going unemployed for long. With his coaching and techniques, I've been able to get several job inquiries and improve my salary within six weeks of coaching. I've greatly improved my resume, job-searching ability, salary negotiating and job interviewing skills. Hire Josef as a career coach, and you won't have to worry about unemployment ever again. At minimum, you should buy his book when it comes out."

Julie Bam
Interactive Developer/Publicist, May 8, 2011, Julie was a client of Josef's.

"I highly recommend Josef's career coaching and resume/cover letter writing services to anyone who is job hunting or looking to change careers. Thanks to Josef, I was recently hired by Apotex Pharmaceuticals, a company I have wanted to work for since my university days. Josef is very good at what he does. His services are amazing!"

JOSEF STETTER

For over 16 years, Josef Stetter has incorporated humour, energy, passion and full self-expression into his personal and professional life.

He is an Award-Winning and International Best-Selling Author in Canada and the USA of *Congratulations You Are Hired: It Was Easier Than You Thought.* Josef also published four other books and is an Award-Winning Speaker and Guinness World Record Participant.

He didn't know what he wanted to do when he grew up, so he switched careers nine times and jobs 17 times. Josef worked in Recruitment, and his clients have included Deloitte & Touche, Aecon Construction, Tata Consulting Services, Canon, Aviva, Skechers Shoes and more!

Josef personally helped over 11,000 people find a job they love with a 90% success rate of finding anyone employment in any field in under three months with proven systems. The fastest he helped someone land a great role was in two days.

Josef Stetter brings forth an interesting twist to getting things done and achieving results that go well beyond expectations.

Josef Stetter helps you take the headache out of navigating the abyss of job searching or hiring by sharing advanced strategies that maximize results. He understands the importance of clear, concise, confident and conversational communication to generate results that are truly unbelievable!!!

You can join Josef on Facebook at:

https://www.facebook.com/groups/landyourdreamjobnow or
https://www.facebook.com/Josef-Stetter-148384127377499

Follow him on Instagram:

https://www.instagram.com/josef_stetter/

Conclusion

Thank you for reading this book. It contains valuable lessons that you can use to become magnetic yourself.

One of the best ways to become magnetic is to become an author and I would love to help you with that. If you would like to be a part of *The Magnetic Entrepreneur* series, please contact me at *magneticpublishing2017@gmail.com* or visit my Business Facebook page *Magnetic Entrepreneur Inc.* Become more than you can ever imagine!

Robert J. Moore
Guinness World Record holder
International Speaker

Internationally Awarded / Bestselling Author of:
  Resilience
  From Rock Bottom to Success and
  The Better Way Formula – Principles for Success and
  Magnetic Entrepreneur

www.ingramcontent.com/pod-product-compliance
Lightning Source LLC
Chambersburg PA
CBHW071140220526
45467CB00015B/1670